JOSH MOODY

# How Church Can Change Your Life

ANSWERS TO THE TEN MOST COMMON
QUESTIONS ABOUT CHURCH

CHRISTIAN
FOCUS

D0423657

paperback ISBN 978-1-78191-611-7
epub ISBN 978-1-78191-626-1
mobi ISBN 978-1-78191-627-8

First published in 2015
by
Christian Focus Publications Ltd,
Geanies House, Fearn, Ross-shire
IV20 1TW, Scotland, UK
www.christianfocus.com

A CIP catalogue record for this book is available from the British Library.

Designed and typeset by
Pete Barnsley (Creativehoot.com)

Printed by Bell & Bain, Glasgow

The New Testament simply has no category for a Christian apart from a church. Christians have always understood that the fellowship of the saints in the context of a local church is God's primary means of discipling his people. Moody has written a powerful and needed reminder of the central role the local church should play in the life of every Christian.

R. Albert Mohler,

President, The Southern Baptist Theological Seminary, Louisville, Kentucky

'Why should I go to church?' This is a question that is being asked today by many Christians, who assume that their faith is primarily about a personal spiritual relationship with God, and also by people who are interested in Jesus but suspicious or unexcited by the idea of institutional religion. Josh Moody faces this challenge head on, recognising that many people love Jesus but are not sure about the church. He answers the top ten questions people have about church simply, clearly and biblically. He presents a compelling case for why we must be part of a healthy local church. This book is short, accessible and easy to read. Each answer is complemented by an accompanying story, and there are helpful questions for discussion. It is ideal for new Christians, seekers who are unsure about the church, and for all those who have lost sight of the glorious truth that the church is God's agency for changing the world.

John Stevens,

National Director, Fellowship of Independent Evangelical Churches

This book answers questions about the church that your friends are asking! In these brief pages Josh Moody helps us understand the relevance of church for believers and nonbelievers too. Read this book and be encouraged by his answers, and then pass it along to a friend who has considered church attendance to be optional.

Erwin Lutzer,
SENIOR PASTOR, MOODY CHURCH, CHICAGO, ILLINOIS

If you want to find truth…., if you want to know hope and give hope to the world…, if you want to live a life of meaning…, if you want help in the Christian life…, if you want to understand truth that changes people…

It is church life that God has given for all of the above and this book will convince you.

This book is just brilliant.

Steve Levy,
PASTOR, MOUNT PLEASANT BAPTIST CHURCH, SWANSEA, WALES

# Contents

Introduction..........................................................................i

1. Is church only for Christians? ...........................................1

2. Do I need to go to church if I am a Christian?...................7

3. Which church is the true church?.....................................15

4. Why are there so many different kinds of churches?.............23

5. What is the point of baptism and communion? ........................31

6. Why is preaching important? ...........................................39

7. Why is there so much politics in church life? ...........................47

8. Should I go back if I have been hurt by church?.......................57

9. What should I look for in a healthy church? ................................65

10. How can I serve in a church?............................................73

Conclusion............................................................................81

# Introduction

Why another book on church?

If you have been following recent publishing trends in Christian circles you will know that there has been a spate of books on church (or 'ecclesiology'). Running through the whole list of titles that have appeared in the last ten years would be boring and redundant; you could google them yourself. But the point is there are a lot of them.

So why another book on church? Because this book is asking a fundamentally different question than the other books that are predominant in publications over the past decade. In fact, that single different question is divided into ten questions in this book for ease of reading. And the overarching question is this: 'Why should I go to church at all?'

Obviously, not many books have been written on that theme because writing a book on church for people who are not sure they want to go to church is a bit like writing a book on writing for people who are not sure they want to write. There's not a big market for books for people who don't like to think about the subjects of the books that are being written. First of all, you have to be interested in church before you are likely to read a book on it. Once you are interested in church, then you will be asking different kinds of questions, namely – as a coverall kind of question – 'How do you do church?'

This is technically called a 'polity' question, that is referring to matters like the organizational structure of how you do church, with particular references to authority structures, roles and the like: 'How do you do leadership?'; 'How do you do membership?'; 'How do you do worship services?'; 'How do you do outreach?'; 'How do you do small groups?' Obviously there is an important market that seeks to engage conversation about these matters.

The conversation has recently shifted, however.

That is because statistics are coming out, as well as anecdotal evidence, which suggests that the rising generation of millennials is asking a different kind of question. In some ways it is the same question that has been asked ever since the anti-institutional revolution came about as a result of Vietnam and the Swinging Sixties. As John Stott began in his famous book *Basic Christianity*, people love Jesus but are not sure about the church.

## Why go to church?

While in some ways, however, this is an old question – 'Why should I bother going to church?' – in other ways it is a new question, or at least a newly asked question. 'Why should I go to church?' That is, 'Why should I be involved in church? What does this thing called the local church have to do with Christianity (or "spirituality")? Can't I just be "spiritual" but not be "religious"?' (which seems at least in part to mean not wanting to have an affiliation with a religious 'institution').

Of course, many of us are suspicious of, or unexcited by, institutions. But more and more people are asking themselves 'Why go to church?' and not just (the topic of most other recent books on church) 'How do you do church?'

This book is an attempt to answer the question 'Why go to church?' It is broken up into ten subsidiary questions – confidently dubbed 'answers to the ten most common questions about church'. Whether they are *the* most common questions I suppose none can say. All I can offer is that in my experience (having now been a pastor for twenty years or so) they are very common indeed. Within these questions there are inevitably answers to some of the questions about how to do church, as well, but the focus is the prior and more foundational question: 'Why should I go to church at all?'

The answer to that would be easy to oversimplify or shove down people's throats in an unsubtle and insensitive way. It would also be easy to say that the answer is simply to make the church more contemporary. I am certainly not opposed to 'bringing the church up–to-date' (though what that means depends on who is proposing it) as long as that does not also mean abandoning what Jesus said, in his Word, the church should be. But my instinct (and experience) is that people are not asking the question 'Why do I need to go to church?' because they are looking for more rock drums (and that comes from someone whose wife is a rock drummer). Smoke machines, dry ice, skinny jeans and laser shows are not wrong. But they are not the answer either.

I first began to discover this misplaced attempt to answer the question when I was working in an area of the world which was considered very secular and postmodern, which, I suppose, meant that not many people went to church anymore. We were exposed to all sorts of ideas from consultants and denominational leaders about how to draw people (back) to church. I listened. I thought. It occurred to me at some point that most of these ideas were the equivalent of trying to persuade people to buy Coca-

Cola (or Pepsi) when the reality was that the people around me had no interest in soft drinks at all. There was no point putting in place a really cool rock band (much as I am in favor of that sort of thing) or building a better car park (again, as much as that can be a good thing to do). But there was no point doing that when people were not coming to church because they thought church *in itself* was pointless. You can't base your argument around the assumption that people want some sort of soft drink and try to persuade them to drink Coca-Cola instead of Pepsi when actually they need first to be persuaded to drink any kind of soft drink in the first place.

The prior questions with relation to church are simply: 'Is it necessary?' 'Do I *have* to go?' Of course, when you put it like that, you immediately cringe. It's a bit like a husband saying to his wife, 'Do I *have* to kiss you?' Something is a bit wrong when that is the question on the table.

So we need then to cast a vision for what the church is, so that the question 'Do I *have* to go to church?' is replaced with, 'What can I do to serve the church?'

The trouble of course is that people's ideas of church are so miscued that if church – biblical church – were really like they think it is, then I don't much blame them staying away.

You see this in marketing all the time. Whenever there is a piece about the church, you will see a picture accompanying it that has two older people and a large empty stone building. The reality is that in many parts of the world, and in many churches, there are booming congregations. Media is selective with its depiction of the reality.

Sometimes it can almost be funny. One church I pastored had in its congregation an average age of about 27. We literally had maybe three people over 65 in the whole place. Our *elders* were in their late 20s. You get the idea. When we finally managed to buy a church building, the local newspaper turned up to capture the big moment. The place was packed with college students. We had a rock band on stage. There was laughter, excitement, a sense of thrill and newness. The news guys didn't come into the building; they didn't even enter. They took one picture – the one that went on the front page of the newspaper – of me at the door hugging one of those three older people. I loved each and every one of those three; hence the hug. But to depict that age range as a true representation of what was going on was extraordinary.

You see this media selectivity over the church worldwide.

On the other hand, people sometimes get wrong ideas about the church for good reasons. If you are one of those, then I am sorry. I know I have not personally hurt you, and my apology won't make a shred of difference in all likelihood. But there it is. Remember Christ died for the church – and boy, does it need saving.

There is another point here, though, before we get into the main body of this book and these ten questions – and that is pride.

The reality is that it is very hard for us to believe that the secret of the universe, the center of the infinite majesty of all reality, the revelation of God in Christ, the Word eternal, is all being discussed in one rather small building on the corner of our street – or even in one very large building in the center of our town.

Why is it like this? To help us, perhaps, we start off how we will need to continue – with humility. Going to church gets us out of our self-oriented prison. We are forced to sit next to someone who reeks of garlic. We are forced to put up with music that is not our taste. We are made to listen to truths that we wish were rather not true. All this is good for us.

It is not only good for us; it is essential if we are to find joy. 'Blessed are the poor in spirit, for theirs is the kingdom of heaven' (Matt. 5:3).

## QUESTION 1

# Is church only for Christians?

It's a little surprising until you come across the idea for the first time, but there are quite a lot of people who think that going to church is something that you should only do if you are a Christian.

After all, I suppose the thinking is that if you are a Muslim, you go to a mosque; if you are Hindu, you go to a temple; and if you are a Christian, you go to a church. If you are not a Christian, or do not believe in any sort of higher power at all, you go to Starbucks on Sunday morning instead. You wash your car. You play golf. You catch up on sleep after a busy week. You read the latest blog on your iPad, and you generally take life easy on Sunday morning.

The strange thing is that some people who do not call themselves Christians feel that if they were to turn up one Sunday morning or

Saturday evening at a church service, they would be intruding. They look around and wonder whether everyone is thinking, 'What are *they* doing here? Surely they know you are meant to bow at this point, raise hands here, scratch behind left ear in meaningful way as the minister performs this particular genuflection?'

The strange thing is that actually many people who are regular church-goers are absolutely *thrilled* when new people decide to show up and check out church for the first time. They don't *care* whether the newcomers know everything or not – they are like a breath of fresh air. They want the new people to have the freedom to find things out, and wish to see if they encounter the God that these regular church-goers believe is real.

Why this feeling then that someone who is not yet a Christian perhaps should not be *allowed* to come to church? Or, if they do turn up, why do they sometimes feel uncomfortable? After all, if you've never been to a natural history museum before, you don't think everyone is thinking, 'What's this guy doing here? You mean he can't tell the difference between a pterodactyl and a brontosaurus! Get him out of here!'

Some of this comes down to the sheer *awkwardness* of many church services. The funniest example of this awkwardness comes from a clip on YouTube of Rowan Atkinson as he plays his well-known comic character Mr Bean. It is sheer comedy gold. The link is http://tinyurl.com/myab7av.

This is also strange because as the late former Archbishop of Canterbury William Temple is said to have put it, 'Church is the one society that exists for the benefit of its non-members.' That is the whole point of church, to be a living testimony to who God is for those who are looking to discover him. The Puritans talked about it in terms of 'means of grace'. The church is a 'means of grace'. It is a zone which God has designed where, if you come with an open heart and if the Spirit is at work in your life, you will encounter God himself. It's not our place; it's his place. It's not a 'sanctuary' in the sense of a special religious area which is separate from normal human reality; it's more like the center of the TARDIS in *Doctor Who*. It's a place where the time orbit of the universe is designed to be able to open up. This 'temple' is really Jesus himself (John 2:20-21), and church is simply a means to that encounter with Jesus.

I remember a conversation I had with someone along these lines. We had gone out kayaking into the Long Island Sound. This is a calm piece of water that extends from New York City into New England and is a precious reserve of wildlife and offers opportunities for water sport. He and his wife had come to visit us, and I was hoping that he might come to church with us. It was a little awkward because I was the preacher, and asking someone to church when you are preaching is a bit like asking someone to a restaurant when you are the cook. You know the conversation after church, if they come, will be a little awkward, too, as they flounder after seeing you now from a somewhat different point of view after hearing you preach the Bible. Anyway, I was trying to build up courage to invite this person to church, and as we paddled around in our kayaks, some sort of garbled sentence blundered out of my mouth. As I stammered away about him coming to church, he said to me something I will never forget: 'I didn't know you would want us to come. Sure, we'll be there. Look forward to it.' And we kept on kayaking.

In other words, no big deal. And in other words, you are invited and welcome, and sometimes people who don't regularly come to church just need to hear that.

3

I asked that person afterwards what he thought of the church. He said some nice things about the sermon (always good to hear), and then he remarked how a particularly square-bodied person had greeted him when he came in the door. He said it was like being hugged by a small car.

## A story

*Bill was not sure he belonged. He walked into the large church building and scanned around. Apparently, he had arrived late as there were no seats at the back of the auditorium – the place to which he naturally would have gravitated. A friendly-looking man smiled at him and offered him a handshake as he hovered on the threshold. Somewhat gingerly he took it – a firm grip, brief look in the eye. He was ushered all the way down the aisle to the front of the church. There wasn't much room for him elsewhere. They were singing some sort of song, words that he could not catch, and once the usher had deposited him in his assigned seat, he attempted to follow along. Before too much time had passed, the song was over, and everyone immediately sat down. After a moment's hesitation, he joined them.*

*Some guy got up to the podium, prayed for a moment or two, opened what Bill was pretty certain was a Bible, and started to speak. He had a gentle manner and was reasonably engaging, and for most of the time Bill was listening.*

*At the conclusion they sang again. Bill joined in once more, now slightly less hesitatingly. The 'service' apparently had now come to an end. He looked around wondering whether anyone would talk to him, and hoping they wouldn't, started to make his way towards the exit. Bill was thinking about God, the Bible, living a life of genuine value – those were some of the themes* that the sermon had encouraged – and he wanted to get out to a coffee shop, order a strong cup of Java and think.

A middle-aged woman accosted him. She had a big smile. Too big, Bill thought, and she began to pump him with questions. How long had he been coming? Where was he from? Was he married? Bill thought the kindly woman was trying to marry him off to her spinster daughter. Before Bill straight out asked what her point was in talking to him, the woman whisked off to have another conversation with someone she evidently knew much better. Bill once more inched his way towards the exit.

Before he could get out, though, the minister reached out a hand to him. 'Thanks for coming', the pastor said. 'Glad you were here.' Bill muttered a reply. What was he to say to a 'man of the cloth'? (Bill thought that was what this kind of person was – not sure – something like that.) Bill hoped that the interview with the minister was over, and he once more (and perhaps at last he would make it) moved towards the door to leave. Before he had taken more than a step, though, the pastor said, 'Anything you would like me to be praying about for you?'

Bill was rooted to the spot. Now that was a question and a half. Anything he would like a man of the cloth to be praying about for him? Was there ever! Not just anything, many things. Bill turned around and this time looked the man in the eye. Before he could stop himself, he began to talk.

## Questions for discussion

1. Do you remember the first time you went to church? What was it like?

2. Do you remember the first time you went to a church that was a different denomination than yours, or was part of a different network than yours? What was that like?

3. When was the last time you went to church?

4. Have you ever been to church? If not, why not? What might help you get involved or at least try out a church for the first time?

5. If you are a church leader, how could you structure your church services in such a way that they maintain biblical fidelity as well as grow in biblical outreach? Are those two values – faithfulness and connection to outsiders – really in contradiction, or does one build on the other?

# Do I need to go to church if I am a Christian?

This is, again, a surprising question, at least historically speaking, but is probably the most prevalent question currently of all ten questions in this book.

Augustine, the great Christian theologian from the fourth and fifth centuries, said, 'There is no salvation outside the church.' Today, certain groups of Christians might instead say, 'There's not much of any salvation in the church.' Today, the mantra is 'Love Jesus … *not quite so sure about the church*.'

This is strange historically; it is even stranger biblically.

Biblically, the church is the body of Christ (1 Cor. 12:27). That means that a Christian is a part of that body. When Paul, the author of the letters to the Corinthians, said that the Corinthian Christians were part of the body of Christ, he was not talking about what theologians term 'the universal church' (that is, the church everywhere and at all times). He meant that actual church in Corinth. '*You*,' he said, writing to the Corinthians, '*you* are the body of Christ.'

To be a member of Christ – that is, to be a real, true Christian – is to be a member of the church. There is no distinction because the church is the body of Christ; therefore, you cannot be a member of Christ without being a member of a church.

People get all hung up about this, because when they think of church, they think of bricks and mortar, and certain complicated religious institutions with hierarchy, and people sitting in big impressive-looking thrones on stages, wearing oddly shaped hats and long white flowing robes, and all that paraphernalia of the traditional church. Obviously, they didn't have much of that in Corinth in the first century when Paul wrote to the Corinthians.

Paul is talking about the organic church, but he also does mean an actual church – an actual local church. To be a Christian is to be a member of one of these churches. The New Testament has no example, not a single one, of a Christian who is not a member of a church.

The early chapters of Acts also provide evidence for this. There, when many people became Christians, not only did they put their faith in Jesus, but they were joined to the church. The two go together (Acts 2:41, 47).

Here is what this does *not* mean. This does *not* mean that going to church saves you all on its own. The joke is so old it is practically hackneyed in church circles, and I can barely prevent myself from yawning as I type it, but it's still effective in its own way: going to church doesn't make you a Christian any more than going to McDonald's makes you a hamburger. Mere institutional allegiance, mere actual physical presence in a church building at a church service, however regular, however devoted in being there every time the church meets, is not what will save anyone. We are saved by faith in Jesus, not by church attendance.

Here is what this *does* mean, however. It means that if you say you follow Jesus but you are not a member of a local church that is biblically founded and gospel-preaching, I have no reason to know for sure whether you actually are following Jesus. In fact, I have pretty good evidence to suggest you are not. Church is the natural expression of someone who follows Jesus in the same way that the natural expression of a hand is to be attached to its body. I might be able to be persuaded that a hand I found wriggling around on the floor detached from a human arm might belong to some real human nearby, but I'd want to rush both the hand and the body off to the hospital pretty quickly for surgery. In fact, I wouldn't feel in good spirits about the prospects unless I found a really good surgeon. Even then, the outcome would be dicey.

Going to church means going to a local church that calls itself a church. This is not the same as listening to an iTunes podcast of praise music in pajamas with a Bible balanced nearby and a coffee at your elbow. There's nothing wrong with doing that, but it's not going to church. Going to church is not the same as hanging out with a bunch of evangelical Christian students in a dorm reading a Bible study with real passion and commitment, and a totally radical mission, and ignoring the older people down the road who desperately need you to come along to encourage and serve them. It is not being so self-absorbed that you can't meet someone outside of your own age group who might have an IQ of less than 120.

If there are good biblical, Jesus-preaching churches nearby, if you are not physically sick and are able to get there, and if you say you follow Jesus, then if you are not a member of one, I have my doubts as to whether you really are following Jesus. You might be just a look-alike, a fake part of the body, rather than a dismembered hand that desperately needs re-attaching.

In short, if you don't go to church, even if you prayed a sinner's prayer at a camp retreat, I think you are in danger. Don't you think that hand that's cut off is in danger of dying, too?

Being a member of a church does not mean simply putting your name in some electronic database and getting annoying mailings and emails. It means expressing in a formal way a personal commitment to a local body of Christ. It's like a wedding ring. In some cultures men do not wear wedding rings; in our culture they do. The formal expression of membership will vary from culture to culture, but the essence is the same. When you become a member and sign on the dotted line, you are making certain commitments, and the formal process is like a wedding ring, showing that you've made that commitment to other fellow believers in the church.

Should you go to a church if you are a Christian? *Yes.*

## A story

*Jane had somehow fallen out of the habit of going to church. It had not been through any conscious decision, as such. But, bit by bit, she realized that she was attending less and less. At first she felt guilty about it. She was busy with* her work, and when it came to Sunday morning, she did not feel like getting up and dressed, then making her way to church. It seemed like too much hassle some weeks. When she had missed a couple of weeks in a row, she realized that there were other things to do on Sunday morning – and some of them were quite fun. She went out to brunch with a friend at a nearby café. There was a whole group of people there, none of them seeming particularly evil. They were eating, chatting and reading newspapers. She and her friend connected really well that morning, and it became a new routine.

Jane still read her Bible from time to time. But church became an occasional chore for when her friend was out of town, or when she found there was some program or event at church that particularly caught her attention.

Gradually, a strange dynamic started to take place. Jane no longer felt guilty when she was away from church. In fact, she felt quite liberated. She signed up for a local running club and got fit again, and she began to go on 5K runs for fun. She was making friends and feeling less exhausted on Monday morning because she had taken the whole weekend off to relax and recharge.

No, she did not feel guilty when she stayed away from church. Actually, now she started to feel guilty when she went to church. It wasn't that the minister's messages were particularly heavy or guilt-inducing, it was just that when she was there she felt like everyone was looking at her saying 'Why aren't you here more often?' That made her feel bad. Jane did not like to feel bad, so she stayed away more frequently.

Things would have stayed like this, in all likelihood, for the rest of her life had she not happened to go to that friend's wedding.

It was a fairly typical wedding: not overly fancy, but done right, in a church, with all the bells and whistles. Jane was actually a bridesmaid. She wasn't married herself yet, and so she was going around thinking about all the preparations and what things she would and wouldn't do when she got married. She liked the bridesmaids' dresses (a revelation: every other wedding she had been to, the dresses for the bridesmaids seemed mainly designed to make the bride look good by comparison). The flowers were not her kind of thing; the music was interesting, different, well done and had some tunes that were drawn from some of her favorite bands playing in the background.

All in all, Jane was having a pretty good time. That is, until the sermon.

The preacher read from Ephesians 5, where Paul says that marriage is a visual image of Christ's love for the church.

That made her think. For some reason she had never really noticed that the church was Jesus' bride.

That was a whole different level of seriousness, significance and conviction. Now she didn't feel guilty about going to church. She also didn't feel guilty about not going to church. She realized that she desperately needed to get back in touch with this bride of Christ.

Jane emailed the pastor's wife when she got home. 'Can we get coffee?' was the subject headline. She realized she didn't need to 'go' to church; she needed to become a part of the church.

For Jane, it started with coffee.

## Questions for discussion

**1.** Why do you think some people reckon they can be Christians without being involved in a local church?

**2.** What does Jesus think when people say they follow him, but they ignore his bride?

**3.** What could your local church do differently in order to present itself as a body and not just as an organization or institution? How could you help make that happen?

**4.** Do you think the idea of 'going' to church needs to be replaced with a different metaphor?

**5.** How could you be more involved with your local church?

**6.** All families are a little dysfunctional. How can you love the more dysfunctional aspects of your local Christian family, the church?

## QUESTION 3

# Which church is the
# true church?

Now we are getting controversial! This is the kind of question that people have gone to war about, which just proves that you shouldn't take questions about God lightly. It also proves that what people have done in the name of religion shows how awful people are, and only occasionally does it show how awesome God is. God's 'brand name' needs some serious re-working on this particular question.

Let's begin at the beginning, or at least with Jesus – which is usually a good place to start. Jesus only talks about the church, using that specific term, twice. That's it, no more than this. That's not to say that the people of God more generally are not at the background to just about everything he is doing (of course, they are). In fact, Jesus' disciples are the church in miniature: twelve disciples for the twelve tribes of Israel (as has been pointed out many times). But Jesus only uses the actual word 'church' two times.

The first occasion is related to Jesus' famous declaration to Peter. Peter has confessed that Jesus is the Christ (Matt.16:15-16). Then Jesus calls him 'Peter' (a kind of nickname; previously he had been Simon, now he was Peter, that is, Rock – you might say he was Rocky Simon). Then after that name-calling (in a positive sense), Jesus says that 'on this rock I will build my church' (Matt. 16:18).

What was Jesus talking about? Books, volumes of discussion and much heated debate have gone into that question. I cannot unravel it all here. I can just tell you my take on it. My opinion is that Jesus means what Peter has said (Jesus is the Christ), not who said it (Peter). The reason I think this is because, right after this moment, Peter then goofs up big time. After having confessed Jesus as the Messiah, he then goes on to tell Jesus not to die on a cross. Jesus then looks at Peter and says, 'Get behind me, Satan!' (Matt. 16:22-23).

Now, what does that mean? Logically, if you say that the first time Jesus meant Peter himself, not what Peter said, then you'd have to say that the second time Jesus meant that, too. So now Peter has been moved from the rock on which Jesus will build the church to the embodiment of Satan himself. Not a bad afternoon's work for a recalcitrant disciple. Impressive stuff, Peter!

Instead, it's far more likely that in the second instance Jesus means the same as he means in the first instance – in both instances Jesus is talking about *what* Peter said. When Peter said Jesus was the Messiah, Jesus is saying that that confession of Jesus is the rock on which he will build his church. And when Peter says to Jesus not to die on a cross, *what* Peter said then is devilish. This means that the foundation, the rock of the church is the message of Jesus Christ and him crucified.

Coincidentally – or not, actually – the apostle Paul said exactly the same thing a little later. He resolved to preach nothing but Christ and him crucified (1 Cor. 2:2) – the power of the gospel – and *that* is the foundation of the church.

So my first answer to 'Which church is the true one?' is that the true church is the one that has at its foundation the proclamation from the Bible of Jesus Christ and him crucified. That's why at our church we have 'proclaiming the gospel' as our vision statement. This is the core foundation of the church.

Jesus, though, mentions the word 'church' one other time. In this instance it is when Jesus is asking how on earth his followers are going to get along and live together in community. The answer is that they have to forgive each other. How are they going to do that if someone sins against them? Well, Jesus gives a three-step plan.

First, go and tell the person his fault, just between the two of you. Keep it private, don't let egos enter in, have a nice friendly chat, and most likely the other person will apologize, and you will then say 'I forgive you,' and all will be hunky-dory again. However, sometimes the person who hurt you won't listen. Well then, second, you go with one or two others to the person.

Now the reason why you bring in one or two others is not to gang up on the person. I've been around in church circles long enough to know that sometimes people use this 'discipline' thing as a way to act vindictively against others. It may turn out that the person making the accusation is the real bad apple here. The two witnesses are there to help discern that. Anyway, then it is usually sorted out.

But if it is not (here comes the word 'church') then, third, Jesus says 'tell it to the church' (Matt. 18:17). So the other mark of a real church is that it takes seriously its responsibility to act in a way that represents what it means to follow Jesus. The church as a community is intended to be able to showcase what it means to follow Jesus authentically.

So the other sign of a true church is that it is a church that is serious about discipleship (and even that intensive form of discipleship: discipline). You can't have a healthy body if you aren't disciplined enough to eat right and exercise. It's the same with body life in church – not weird, freaky stuff as in some religious sect, but healthy body life, like going to the gym and cutting out the cigarette chain-smoking – meaning not being nasty to each other and also forgiving one another.

There's one other sign of the true church, and that is the way it deals with baptism and communion. We'll come to that in Chapter 5.

In short, if you want to find a true church you are looking for three things. You are looking for the true preaching of Jesus Christ and him crucified. You are looking for healthy discipleship and discipline. Also, you are looking for the way that the church does baptism and communion to be biblical.

That's it. You're not looking for perfection. You're not looking for really cool music. You're not looking for a mix between Billy Graham, John Chrysostom, Charles Spurgeon and your favorite preacher that you podcast on your iPhone. You are looking for the gospel, discipleship and the right way of doing baptism and communion.

That's the church, the true church. It's not what kind of hierarchy you have, how tall your steeple is, and if you know the funny handshake or all the insider jokes about the nursery worker who once got lost on his way from one classroom to another.

## A story

*Gerald had always been told that his church was the true church. It didn't strike him at the time as a particularly unusual thing to say – after all, everyone thought that their 'thing' was the best. Why shouldn't church feel that it was the real deal, too? As he listened more and more, though, to the teaching and approach of this very small fellowship in the country, he realized that when they said that their church was the true church, what they meant was that no other church was.*

*That, Gerald realized, was a different order of claim. It was one thing to be confident that what you did was the right thing to do. It was another to claim that what anyone else did was wrong by definition because it was not exactly what you did. Surely, Gerald began to wonder, there must be some overlap between their basic principles and the basic principles of other churches. Even if they did disagree on some matters, surely there were things that they held in common. The leaders of Gerald's church began to treat him differently and look at him with a tinge of concern, more as if he was a 'project' to be worked on than a person to work with.*

*Gerald began to wonder out loud what it was that made a church a true church. Was it the preaching? Was it the music? Was it the personality of the pastor? Was it the leadership? Was it the history of the church? What defined a church as a real church, and what defined a religious gathering as not actually a true church?*

*Fortunately for Gerald, an elderly gentleman at his very small church happened to hear him having this conversation with a friend in the vestibule after a service one day. The elderly gentleman hobbled over to Gerald, leaning on a cane, and with a twinkle in his eye smiled at him and said, 'My friend, you ask good questions!' Gerald was transfixed. Here was someone who wanted to talk. They sat together and began to chat away for five minutes or so before Gerald left to go home. In that time the elderly gentleman said very little and listened very much. At the end he said a surprising thing: 'You know, you might like to try reading the book of Hebrews. They were wrestling with something similar.'*

*Gerald had heard of Hebrews, had read it, but had never heard a sermon on it. The book struck him as particularly irrelevant to modern life, all about priests and temples and sacrifices and various Old Testament religious paraphernalia. How on earth could this book answer his question? Still, he liked the old man who made the suggestion, so he decided to give it a try.*

*After he had finished reading it, following a couple of hours or so of careful perusal, Gerald sat back, looked up at the ceiling and thought. And thought. Clearly, the book was about the importance of 'the Word'. The readers were being asked to listen to that Word very carefully. Clearly also the book was about 'not giving up meeting together', and it was calling the readers to keep on gathering as a church – and not to go back to the synagogue. Clearly also there was a heavy emphasis on faith, the heroes of faith, as well as on discipline, serious discipleship.*

*Was that all there was to it? Gerald began to wonder whether church could be defined in the way that Hebrews defined it. About the gospel, or the Word, and faith in that Word. About discipleship and discipline and serious committed gathering together. Was that all there was?*

*The next Sunday he saw the old man again and asked him whether he thought he had understood the book correctly.*

*'Sounds about right', the elderly gentleman wheezed to him kindly.*

*'What, then', said Gerald, 'is there nothing else that defines a true church?'*

*'There is one other thing', the old man said.*

*'What's that?' asked Gerald.*

*'Well', he replied, 'now you might try reading what Jesus says about the church in the Gospels. Search for it and see what he specifically says about church. Make sure you include his last words to his disciples at the end of Matthew's Gospel.'*

*Gerald did the research. He came across the Lord's Supper and baptism. The old man had said there was 'one other thing', so perhaps they somehow went together as sacraments or ordinances.*

*'Is that right?' he asked the elderly gentleman next time saw him. 'Is It the Word, discipleship and the ordinances?' The man shuffled past him nodding gently.*

*Gerald sat down for the service. He went out feeling as if he was clear about some things that before had always bothered him. The rest of the people began to find him less of a project, too.*

*When he left home, it meant he tried out some other churches, different denominations from the tiny little group which he now called 'his home church' (rather than 'the only church'). But he appreciated what he had learnt – especially from the elderly gentleman – and realized that if he found the Word, discipline and the ordinances – all with biblical framing – then he was present in a real true church.*

## Questions for discussion

1. Have you come across churches that think they have the truth and no one else does?

2. How do you encourage people to realize the core identity of a true church?

3. What in your mind makes a church a true biblical church?

4. Does the church you currently attend, or the one you would like to attend, display these elements of a true biblical church?

5. Why do you think churches have sometimes claimed that other elements of their ministries are essential to being a true church?

6. Why is it that some so-called churches do not have biblical teaching, discipline and the ordinances?

# Why are there so many different kinds of churches?

I wish there were more churches, at least true biblical churches. The fake kind I'd like to remove surgically from the face of the planet immediately!

What's behind this question ('Why are there so many different kinds of churches?') is usually the thought that it shows: that the church is disunited, and therefore somehow witnesses against the truth of the church as an expression of God today. Those who know their Bibles might even mention John 17, where Jesus prays that the church would be *one*. 'How come it's not?' they might then ask.

But really, this is all a fairly massive misunderstanding: both of the value of having lots of different kinds of churches, and of Jesus' prayer. Jesus prays that his disciples would be one as he and the Father are one. He does not pray that they would all be able to fit into the same box, like having the same music or architecture, wearing the same clothes and being part of the same institution. He never prays any of that, which is probably a good thing, because to achieve that would take a miracle almost as big as walking on water every day.

No, the point of Jesus' prayer is *relational*, not *institutional*. To be one as Jesus and the Father are one is a *relational* oneness. Jesus is part of the Trinity – he is fully God and fully man in one person. Christians believe that God is one in three persons: God the Father, God the Son (Jesus) and God the Holy Spirit. Therefore, what Jesus means is that we are to be one like that. It is a relational oneness, a oneness like the way really good friends are one even though they are different people, or like the way husband and wife are one even though sometimes they annoy each other. The husband just loves to watch *Rocky III* movie re-runs over and over again, and the wife just loves to sit down with a box of Kleenex and watch some Jane Austen 'chick flick' with her girlfriends. They are not *institutionally* one; they are *relationally* one.

I believe the church, as we defined it in Chapter 3, is one right now all around the world.

I've experienced this over and over again – every day, in a way. My ancestors were not on the *Mayflower*. I am not from the South Side of Chicago; I did not go to Wheaton College; and I had never seen the prairies until I was 18. I still don't understand baseball completely. Despite all this, I am one with other Christians who are all these things, and they with me. We are one in Christ – Jew and Gentile, slave and free, all nations in Christ.

I've also experienced it travelling around the world. You're dumped in some little village in the middle of nowhere, and you stumble into a church. The Bibles are open and someone is preaching Christ crucified, and *you are family*. That's what it feels like, because that's the reality. You are one with them in Christ.

Honestly, I think all the different churches are really a good thing. Can you imagine what it would be like if we all had to agree precisely on the same this, that or the other? I mean, we can go to some big conference and put up with the way things are done for a day or two, but every week, all the time? No way.

It's good as long as we remember that we are one with the Baptists down the road, the Presbyterians up the road, the Anglicans, even those rather strange people who meet in that little small building with the vestibule that still smells of the previous minister's rotting socks – yes, even with those who truly believe in Christ who come from different denominations than we do. Our unity is in Christ, not in church, and therefore we are truly one even if our church tastes are different. All these different churches give Jesus a bigger reach because they help us connect with different kinds of people.

It would be rather sad, I think, if church instead was like some massive chain restaurant or outlet, a franchise where everything would be exactly the same. If it were like that, we'd need to create different kinds of franchises because some people like McDonald's and, well, some people don't. They prefer Wendy's, and on and on it could go.

Why are there so many different kinds of churches? Probably because there are quite a number of different kinds of people. While you love all the other Christians, you don't want to have to share a house with them – not all of them, not all of the time. That's okay. It's probably actually a good thing. It stops us from fighting each other.

## A story

*Isaiah had grown up in a Christian Missionary Alliance church. It had been a small but happy church, and he had learnt a lot about God and the Bible. Once he graduated from high school Isaiah went away to college, and there was no Christian Missionary Alliance church near the university campus. So he began to explore his options.*

*Soon enough he was hit by a bewildering array of different choices. There was the Baptist church; in fact there were several of them, with different names which didn't make it clear to him whether they were all related, or whether they had quite different beliefs. There was the Methodist church, then, of course, the Anglican church, but then also another church which was Episcopalian, and that seemed different from the Anglican. After a while trying these different options, a few of Isaiah's friends took him to a church that was called by the name of a river nearby. It didn't seem to have any particular denominational affiliation at all – or if it did you wouldn't have known it. This church was massive and complicated, and Isaiah loved it, but also felt a little lost. Where did he belong? He started to explore Roman Catholic churches, too, which, while all part of one great corporation, also had, Isaiah discovered, all sorts of different takes on how to do various things and were called by different names of various saints. All in all, Isaiah was confused.*

*He remembered learning in Sunday school how Jesus had prayed for the unity of his disciples. Had Jesus' prayer not been answered? The church seemed self-evidently not to be unified. In the main, everyone at the different churches that Isaiah explored were polite to each other, though sometimes there were a few snide remarks or a quiet sense of superiority. Isaiah, however, found that the different churches were usually pleasant about each other. But there were still all these different churches with their different names, emphases, worship styles and teachers. Which was right? And why were there so many different ones anyway – especially as Jesus had prayed that his followers 'may be one' as he was one with God the Father. That seemed a pretty high stakes prayer. If the unity of the church was based upon the unity of the Trinity, what did it say about God if his people were not one as he was one? Was he incapable of making them one? Was there yet another church out there which was truly one, and all these other ones were abhorrent to it? That didn't seem to make any sense either.*

*Isaiah found that certain churches felt they were the one true church, and other churches had left it behind. That made him start to read church history. He discovered that not only were there Roman Catholic churches, but there were also Orthodox churches, several different kinds of them united in common confession and history. There were also non-Roman churches that were Catholic – Ukrainian Catholic churches. There were Armenian Apostolic churches which were very ancient, too. There were churches in Southern India that traced their origin, they claimed, to Thomas. There were Celtic churches in Britain that went back before the beginning of Roman Catholicism in that country.*

*The more he read about church history, the idea of finding a single stream of the one true church organizationally seemed incredibly unlikely – quite irrational, he felt.*

*Where to go? If he said, as he realized his own denominational history would have said about itself, that it was based on Scripture, then he also realized that there were many different interpretations of Scripture, hence all the different churches.*

*Isaiah, for a while, felt quite bereft. Perhaps the whole thing was a pack of cards? This was until a friend of his, Isabel, happened to make a remark to him over lunch one day. 'Perhaps', she said, after Isaiah had unburdened himself talking to her, 'organizational unity is not always the real kind of unity.' Isabel went off and left Isaiah's mind whirring silently.*

*He thought of when his family from a different state came to visit him – Aunt So-and-So, Uncle Such-and-Such, a cousin or two or three. There was something about family that connected, even if he did not know them that well. Perhaps real Christians, those truly in the family, really were connected and somehow knew it when they met each other, read the Bible together, prayed together. Perhaps they were one as the Father and Son were one, spiritually one, in truth and in fact. After all, he knew that many organizations that were institutionally one had no kind of real unity at all.*

*Isaiah went on a mission trip that year. He was in the Middle East. He wandered into a very small church in a very small city. He had no idea what label it carried. There was a sermon. There was singing. And there was love. He did not know these people. Their translator made sense of some of what was being said, enough for some communication. And they hugged him, and they prayed together.*

*He was welcomed like a long lost relative. He was family, and so were they.*

## Questions for discussion

**1.** Do you find all the different denominations off-putting?

**2.** Did you grow up in a church, and, if so, what did you think of that church?

**3.** How many different branches of Christendom can you count: Protestant, Catholic, Orthodox, but also Armenian Apostolic, Ukrainian Catholic, and ancient churches like the Celtic church?

**4.** When did you first notice that you were one in Christ with another Christian (if you are a Christian)? What was that experience like?

**5.** Do you think you can be one with another Christian and not feel it? What kind of objective standards of unity should Christians use? (Look at the confessions of faith in 1 Corinthians 15, for instance, or the church confessions like the Apostle's Creed, or the Westminster Confession and others.)

**6.** Have you been part of a large organization that did not seem 'one'? What could be done about it? How does Ephesians 4 encourage us to fight for the 'unity of the Spirit'?

# What is the point of baptism and communion?

When you go to church one of the first things you realize is that this is not exactly like any other meeting you might attend. Churches have some of their own rituals, and I don't just mean the mediocre coffee that is normally served after the service has finished, or the strange assumption that everyone knows exactly what to do at any particular point, or the rather aromatic odor of faintly rotting vegetables emerging from the corridor, or the odd names given to various portions of the building (such as 'nave'). If you keep coming, on some special occasion when you are there, likely as not a baby will get dripping wet and howl with indignation from the front while wearing a badly fitting white outfit that was handed down from grandma, or there will be a line of people waiting to go to the altar, or small plastic cups of red juice will be passed around. For those in the know these are called 'baptism' and 'communion'. Who knew, huh?

As you get into it some more, you will realize that people have all sorts of different theories as to which kind of people should get wet and when, and exactly how much water should be used, and whether the red juice should be passed around in small plastic transparent cups, or distributed from the front in big gold-looking chalices, and any number of variations on the theme. But basically, you will notice that there are these two things called 'baptism' and 'communion'. To make matters even more confusing, some people call them 'sacraments', and other people call them 'ordinances'. What exactly are these things? Why do Christians do them? Do they matter? And if they do, what is the right way that they should be done?

Given that there are HUGE books written on this subject, I don't think I can say enough to satisfy anyone (and certainly not everyone). Basically, though, here are the things to bear in mind, in an ABC of baptism and communion.

**A.** These are *church* things. They are designed to be the entrance to the church (baptism) and the expression of ongoing involvement within the church (communion). They are not for random nice feelings on a beach at sunset with some good friends, or on a college campus with a bunch of like-minded 18-year-olds, or anywhere else that isn't actually a local church.

**B.** These things have a particular *meaning*. Baptism is an expression of being born into the Christian family by the Spirit of God. When you are born of the Spirit you die to your old way of life and you rise to a new life in Jesus. Baptism is an outward expression of this inward reality. Communion is a sign of what Jesus has done on the cross. It was designed by Jesus to help us remember that what he did on the cross was enough to take away all our sins. We are great at beating ourselves up with guilt trips. Communion is intended to say that Jesus' death was enough.

**C.** A lot of the other distinctions – and there are many – about these two matters are fine, and worth considering and getting straight in your own head, but are not to be divisive between Christians. Some things the family does not have to see exactly identically, in the same way that families might like different movies, food and clothes, and still get along just fine. Families need to focus on the truth of who they are as a family – one family together – and love each other. They are not to get all bent out of shape if Johnny likes Super Bowl parties and Annie can only just prevent herself from screaming every time a sports game appears on the TV. You know, we get along despite some of these distinctives without making a big deal about them.

The challenge with both of these things – baptism and communion – is actually at a more basic level still. They are both 'signs', that is, they are designed to point somewhere, but signs if they are not interpreted can easily become misunderstood. I remember this from when I was travelling in various countries. I would come across a sign on a road or a street, and it was clearly apparent that its meaning was obvious to the locals, but we foreigners had no idea what the sign meant. We knew it meant something, but what? Clueless.

Often you have the same issue with baptism and communion. People love signs. The signs feel significant (sort of mystical and mysterious), but because signs by themselves don't say much of anything, if they are not interpreted, when you actually ask people what is going on, or what they mean, they usually do not have a clue. No idea at all. They could not explain it – but, 'Wow, it is like deep, man, oh yeah, *so* deeeep.'

This is why the best way to think of baptism and communion is as 'visible words'. That helps explain how they function in relation to the Bible and to the preaching and teaching of the Bible. They are designed to be visible signs pointing to the same reality that has just been explained. Without that they become signs pointing all over the place, rather than pointing in one particular direction. Baptism says: the way to be saved is to humble yourself, put your trust in Jesus, and then you will come to experience new life now and forever. But it needs to be explained first. Then, when you see the sign, it becomes doubly meaningful. You get the 'visible word' as well as the Word. Communion says: Jesus has died for your sins, once for all; don't forget it, don't ever forget that his death was sufficient and has covered everything. But it also needs to be explained first. Then, when you see the sign of communion, it too becomes doubly meaningful. You get the 'visible word' as well as the Word taught.

In short, baptism and communion are not as complicated as some have made them out to be. Get baptized, take communion – in the local church – as an expression of your faith in Jesus.

## A story

*Barry was somewhat nonplussed when he first saw communion taking place. At a point in the service everyone was encouraged, row by row, to walk down the aisle and then kneel before the altar rail to receive a cracker and then a carefully dispensed sip of communion wine. Barry quite liked the experience, though he wasn't sure he should have been doing it. Was he meant to partake in this at this point given he was so new to Christian things?*

*Later, he went to a different church and they too had communion. The way they did it, though, was entirely different. Instead of everyone getting out of their seats, specially selected individuals at a prearranged moment brought a tray of crackers, and then after a tray of clear plastic cups containing what Barry assumed was some sort of grape juice. This was an equally interesting experience for Barry though, again, he wasn't sure he was meant to be partaking at this early stage of his Christian walk.*

*Another time he went to a church where people stood in line at different parts of the building and received communion at different 'stations'. It was all a bit confusing.*

*The next time Barry went to church he decided he would listen with particular care to the explanation that preceded the communion part of the service – if there was a communion that day. As he listened he began to realize that this ceremonial meal was not merely meant to be mystically intoxicating, but actually to communicate something about the real message of the gospel. It was a reminder, a sign, a celebration, a special moment where he was to remember what Jesus had done, and Jesus by his Spirit was to minister to him. He was to confess his sins. He was to fix his mind on the elements of the cup and the bread. The minister at the time told them all to look, especially with care at the cup and the bread – shed for you, he said of the cup; broken for you, he said of the bread. The meaning in these elements, their message, started to impact Barry more and more profoundly.*

*The next Sunday there was a baptism. This was an adult baptism, though Barry had also seen children baptized. The person being baptized gave his tes-*

timony of how he had become a Christian. Having learnt from his communion experience to pay careful attention to what was being said, Barry listened to the explanation. This water was not going to save the individual, he heard. He was being baptized because he had already been saved. This baptism was an outward sign of an inward work, and it symbolized his dying with Christ and rising again to newness of life. The baptism, as he stared at the individual's 'death' and 'resurrection', was especially meaningful to Barry.

Before long he decided that he should be baptized. During the baptism class he learnt that communion was probably best taken after someone had been baptized, as communion was a sign of being in communion with other baptized Christians. He also learnt more about the gospel.

When the day came for his baptism, Barry was excited. He gave his testimony. Went down into the water. Came up again. Dripping wet.

Afterwards, once he had changed, he was asked what the experience was like. 'It was a bit wet', said Barry. But now that he knew he had already died with Christ, his determination to fight sin was stronger than ever – as was his assurance that he would rise to newness of life on the other side of the grave.

## Questions for discussion

1. How can you prepare yourself for communion?

2. In your own words what does it mean for communion to be a 'visible word'?

3. Have you been baptized? If not, would you consider it? If you have been baptized, in what way does your baptism encourage you now?

4. What parts of the meaning of baptism and communion are biblically essential and non-negotiable? What interpretations are secondary and peripheral and matters over which Christians may legitimately disagree without breaking fellowship?

5. Why do you think Christ ordained baptism and communion? Why was it important for us to 'remember' through these signs?

# Why is preaching important?

Now you are starting to scratch where I itch!

At preaching conventions you will sometimes have a whole bunch of preachers on the platform, giving announcements or making introductions, and then you will have the main preacher doing the main preaching thing. An old joke, and its many funny variations, center around the fact that you just know that with all those preachers on the platform the event is going to go on for *ages*. Most preachers have the gift of the gab, and when you give them the microphone they are going to be especially 'burdened' and 'passionate' and 'convicted in the Spirit' to go on and on forever like some intemperate windbag. By the time the main preacher gets his chance to do the gig he was asked to do, you could have heard several 'sermons' already – called welcome, introduction, prayer, announcements and the like.

Why is preaching important? Or is it just that preachers are self-important? Is preaching the impartation of lots of heavy theological jargon down the throats of the unwilling average, poor church member? Or is preaching instead a whole bunch of really funny jokes strewn together to make people laugh and feel good before sending them on their way (but not before they have appropriately added to the collection plate as it was passed around)? Is preaching something that was invented later in the church, or does it go back to something intrinsic or central to the Bible?

Preaching is important because it is how God speaks today to his people through the Bible. Here is one definition of preaching, from a book I have written with a friend on the subject: 'Preaching is the God-ordained means by which he meets with his people through his Word and by his Spirit in such a way that his people's eyes are opened to see Jesus and be captivated by him.'

So that means:

- Preaching is *not* a bunch of funny jokes stuck together for maximum humorous impact.

- Preaching is *not* a whole mass of theological content downloaded to educate everyone, willing or not.

- Preaching *is* God's way of meeting with people to show them Jesus, so that they are thrilled by him.

In short, the reason why preaching is important is that Jesus is important. I don't just mean that 'Jesus was a preacher, too' (though, of course, he was, which should be something of a hint about the importance of preaching).

I mean that Jesus has set up preaching to show us himself and help us see how great he is. The more you love Jesus, the more you will love preaching.

Preaching, therefore, is not only an information download. Preaching is teaching, but it is more than teaching. Preaching is motivation, but it is more than motivation. It is, when genuine, God addressing us through his Word, the Bible, to show us the beauty of Jesus.

Now, of course, not all preaching is like that. Some preaching is boring, but more to the point some preaching is simply plain wrong. Some preaching is merely a download of information. Even worse, some preaching is attempting to download information that is not biblical.

But biblical preaching is important because it is Jesus' way to meet with his people and show us his glory, his beauty, his love, and to help us be captivated by who he is.

Some things follow from this definition of preaching.

**1.** We should come to hear preaching not merely with a desire to learn more stuff, but with a desire to encounter Jesus. You are listening not to find out whether this guy is saying something new or more exciting than the other guy you heard on the TV or radio, but you are listening as if you were discerning what it is that Jesus wants to say to you. This will forever change your attitude to preaching. I have listened to some terrible sermons (from a technical point of view, and I'm not encouraging technically terrible sermons, by the way) that nonetheless have led me to an encounter with Jesus. And I have listened to technically competent sermons (from a communication standpoint, not a content standpoint) that have utterly failed to point me, or anyone else that I can discern, to Jesus at all. In fact, I have listened to a lot of sermons that have never even mentioned the name of Jesus, let alone made much of Jesus in the hearing of those who are listening.

**2.** We should leave from having heard biblical preaching with a desire to do something about what we have just heard. Jesus makes this point at the end of the most famous sermon ever given, the Sermon on the Mount: 'Therefore everyone who hears these words of mine and puts them into practice is like a wise man who built his house on the rock' (Matt. 7:24). There's no point being shown Jesus in all his beauty and being moved to embrace him anew as the Lord of your life, and then doing absolutely zilch about it. You might as well have not listened at all. In fact, eternally speaking, you would have been better off without the opportunity to hear and to reject what you heard.

**3.** We should pray for and support our preacher. Do it before he preaches as he preaches, and after he preaches. If preaching is this important, you want to gather around the preacher, not to idolize him (God forbid – that would not be making much of Jesus, but making much of preaching or even much of the preacher), but to keep the channel of preaching as clean and as open to the work of the Spirit as possible. It's not your job to be policeman, counselor or person to whom the preacher is accountable, but you do want to be a cheerleader and a fan. Critics can sharpen preachers; God uses opposition, and that can be good for the preacher, and good for those to whom he preaches. But it's not good to have a critical spirit; you don't want to be one of them.

**4.** We should advocate for and ensure that there is enough time, space and resources for the continued development of excellence in preaching.

Churches are not meant to be led by administrative geniuses with fancily marketed programs for all ages; they are meant to be led by Christ through his Word, which means that preaching is centrally important.

## A story

*Elizabeth had a confession to make: she found preaching boring. As soon as someone began, her mind started to drift – almost uncontrollably – to what was on TV last night, and her hand started to long to check her Facebook stream on her phone. 'Channel surfing', she called it. The person could be talking about 'x' biblical doctrine, but her mind would be surfing through Hawaii or California or climbing up some beautiful mountain. Once or twice she even found herself starting to balance her bank account in her head while listening to a sermon. It seemed to be only one step removed from counting sheep – in this instance to keep her awake, rather than to send her to sleep.*

*So Elizabeth decided enough was enough. Obviously, Christians believed that preaching was important. Jesus was a preacher, after all, as were Paul and Peter. In fact, when Elizabeth began to think about it, there weren't that many parts of the Bible (the Bible she loved) that could not be said to have been derived from some sort of original homiletical form or other – perhaps the Psalms (but then that made her think of church music, and Elizabeth found some church music as equally queasy-making as preaching).*

*If, as Elizabeth realized now must be the case, preaching was so important to the Christian faith, it seemed that she should do her level best to understand why. Why preach? Why not have discussions about the truth? Why not have quiet exploration and reflection with music playing in the background? Why this heralding of the truth?*

*Elizabeth knew full well that there were preachers who were better than others. Some, she understood, were even quite famous in their own way and according to their own tribes, but this did not by itself win Elizabeth over to being a fan of preaching per se. She wanted to know why it was so important. It was one thing to be a motivational speaker, or to be able to 'connect' and tell funny stories, or to be engaging in a sort of after-dinner-speech way, but to preach was by its nature saying something different.*

*In fact, as Elizabeth reflected on it, preaching seemed to be saying the sort of thing that culture today especially did not want to be said. It seemed to be saying not just, 'Here is some information, let me help you learn it.' If that was all that preaching was saying, then there were plenty of educational developments that could usefully be employed. After all, why not use a computer-generated smart board during the sermon? Why not show a video of someone doing what you were talking about? Why not have people interact over the matter and discuss it around tables? Why not have people fill out questions and be marked afterwards on how well they did? All these and other methods of education could be employed, if preaching was simply a matter of imparting information or helping people to learn facts.*

*But evidently it was more than that, or different from that, because preaching seemed to be saying (something which our culture did not want to be said) that there was a standard of truth that was decided in a democratic form. This truth was delivered from on high. It almost (symbolically sometimes) came down from the mountain and was handed to you, she felt, like Moses receiving the Ten Commandments, or Ezra reading from the Book of the Law from an elevated platform, or Paul preaching, or Jesus delivering his Sermon on the Mount. Preaching, by its very nature, was saying that God has a Word to deliver, a Word that is our job to receive, believe and rejoice in.*

*Once Elizabeth got her mind around this basic truth about preaching – and about preachers in the Bible and in current times as well – she started to find she had a different attitude to the preacher. She knew that the preacher in the pulpit was no more or less human than she was, and was certainly not sinless either, but that the preaching act was not about the preacher. He was a messenger with a message, not a personality with a product he had invented and was trying to sell. This made Elizabeth more in tune with what was actually taking place. And it made her listen.*

*She still had her 'favorite' preachers, people she found it particularly easy to listen to and especially helpful. She realized, when she started to compare notes with her friends, that to her surprise this list was not the same for everyone. Evidently some preachers were more one person's 'cup of tea' than another's. But while she still found some preachers easier to listen to than others, for whatever reasons of personality or style that may have been present, she now began to appreciate the actual preaching act.*

*In fact, one time listening to a sermon that she knew by any objective sense was not a great sermon – it was poorly structured, and did not have much verbal punch to it – she still found herself rejoicing. Here was someone telling her a message – a message from God – about her salvation, God's love for her, and his deliverance of her from her sins.*

*All at once, for Elizabeth, preaching became not bad news but good news.*

# Questions for discussion

1. What sort of preaching would you say is true preaching? Is there a difference between biblical preaching and unbiblical preaching?

2. What would help you come better prepared to hear preaching?

3. How can you pray for the person who preaches at the church where you attend?

4. How can you support the person who preaches at the church where you attend?

5. There are many resources for learning how to preach: *Burning Hearts* is one that I have recently written with a friend. How could you benefit from reading these resources even if you are not yourself a preacher?

6. Why is it important that churches have expositional preaching – that is preaching that preaches the main point of the passage as the main point of the sermon?

# Why is there so much politics in church life?

Good question! Why indeed? Of course, I immediately could get a little defensive and say, 'Well, there is politics in every area of life, and that is not necessarily bad. Political organization of some kind is an inevitable expression of human organization and social interaction.' I could also say that many churches of which I have been a part have had blissfully little in the way of political shenanigans.

I could say all that, but you and I both still know what the question means. Why is it that there seems to be *even in church* (which is supposed to be so holy and wonderful) personal and social interactions which can be at times painful, and even sometimes give rise to suspicions of political shady goings-on worthy of a minor sub-committee in some back room or other. The answer to this question is that it shouldn't surprise us *and* it shouldn't satisfy us.

It shouldn't *surprise* us because this is exactly what the church has always been like in some way or other. If you read the New Testament, you will find that most of the letters in the New Testament are written in response to some problem in the church to which it is written. You might say that if there weren't any politics in church life, our New Testament would be about half the size, or even smaller, to be honest.

Some Christians look at Jesus' teaching about the parable of the wheat and the weeds (Matt. 13:24-30) and say that this means that even in church life there are those who are not really Christians growing up alongside those who really are Christians, and that we shouldn't try to discern which is which, but just let them grow up together until God decides at the end. Other Christians think that Jesus is talking about the world, not the church, and that we can't decide exactly who are Christians and who are not, but God will judge in the end, and we should let him do it for that is his job. Either way, we have a situation whereby we cannot expect perfection here.

In many ways, this whole question is an *eschatological* issue. That is, it is an issue about the last days and how we understand where we are in God's plan for the whole universe. What we have to grasp is that while Christ has come, and the church is built upon that confession of Christ as Lord, we still live in a 'now-and-not-yet' time. There are still problems and difficulties and politics – and people who really annoy us by singing loudly and often and flat (and such annoyance that we find is an expression of our tendency to feel annoyed by people).

So we shouldn't be *surprised* to find churches less than perfect and to have issues in them. It's what churches were like in the New Testament; it's what Jesus knew they were going to be like (look at all those disciples squabbling about who would be the greatest among them in the Gospels); and it's an expression of the reality that while we are in Christ, we are not in heaven ... yet.

However, though this should not *surprise* us, at the same time it should also not *satisfy* us. We should be aiming for our churches to grow in godliness, in Christlikeness, in love for each other, in simple humble appreciation of each other, in the ability to submit to one another out of reverence for Christ, for that is love. Love for God. Love for his Word. Love for each other. Love for the people around us. In the same way that we should not be satisfied that we are not (yet) who we are meant to be as Christians *individually*, so we should not be satisfied that churches are not (yet) who they are meant to be as Christian communities. We should aim to be presented without spot or blemish, holy and pure, without stain or wrinkle: that is, full of Christ and full of his love.

If it should not satisfy us, how should we go about improving? Here is my list of suggestions, in no particular order, some of which may seem a little idiosyncratic or even counter-intuitive, but I have found these to be helpful in churches, as well as being solidly biblical.

First, I think we all need to chill a little. A lot of stress and strain in church life results from people being too intense. God is a pretty intense topic of conversation. Sometimes that spills into our human interactions, so we relate intensely to each other all the time. If *everything* is of eternal significance, pretty soon everyone gets a bit jumpy. Sometimes it's okay to sit back, read a good book, watch a movie, grab a coffee and talk about football, or ice cream, or the scientific consensus around the unified theory of everything ... you know, whatever gets you going.

Second, I think it is important that the Word is not only theoretically central to church life but functionally central. A lot of issues emerge when something else becomes central, perhaps a human personality, or a particular theory about how to do church, or a particular approach to how to rear children, or whatever is the latest hot button issue in Christian subculture. All that is bound to cause friction because no one ever completely agrees on it. That's okay. We need to talk about stuff that not everyone agrees on, otherwise our lists of things we can talk about would be pretty small. But that stuff, that secondary stuff, cannot be either theoretically or functionally central. That means we have to leave time for the explanation of the Bible, and to have that at the heart of what happens when we meet in big gatherings, as well as in small ones. That's why I always get nervous when the latest Christian book (fad) is the thing that people are studying. Maybe it's a good book, but no, let's study the Bible, not the latest Christian book – which some people will love and others will hate.

Third, love. Love. Love. Love. The Bible says that love covers a multitude of sins. It's amazing what churches can get away with if they just love each other. That doesn't mean we have to like each other. I can love someone without liking them. I can find someone frustrating, or dislike his taste in clothes, but still genuinely and truly want what is best for that person. That's what it means to love someone: to seek what is his or her best. Love does not mean avoiding tough conversations, or not doing any life-on-life accountability, but it does mean that all those sorts of things are not from an arrogant position, but from a loving, humble, gracious, self-giving position. That changes everything; it changes how we speak, and it changes how we listen. Jesus said you could tell his disciples by how they love one another (John 13:35), and so we who are loved by him love each other in turn.

Fourth, true Christians join the membership of the church. In the judgment of charity, as much as we can discern, we want to make sure that the members of the church are actually regenerate, true followers of Jesus. If that is in place, then most other things go much easier, for fairly obvious reasons.

Fifth, leadership. It really matters who churches have in leadership, as elders and pastors, and we need to be careful to pick good ones, encourage them and support them.

With these five elements – not intense; with the Word functionally central; with love; with regenerate membership; and with biblical, excellent leadership – we will gradually grow in our Christlikeness as his church.

We will not avoid all problems. We will not avoid all difficulties. But we will become more like Christ – and less like the world of politics.

## A story

*It was the church meeting to end all church meetings. Dave walked out feeling angry. He had come to the church 'business' meeting (one of his friends quipped that given the church wasn't selling anything he wasn't sure why it had any 'business' meetings at all) filled with hope for some of the exciting things that he had heard that the church was talking about in this season. To be honest, he wasn't sure that all of them were that good of ideas. Some seemed a bit outlandish, and perhaps too 'risky' for the rather risk-averse, conservative-minded, middle-class, middle-aged people who would likely attend the actual meeting. But when Dave thought of the community in which the church was placed – the new high rise buildings that had gone up not a five-minute drive away from the church building, the posh condos, as well as some of the poverty needs in other parts of the town – he was so excited that the church leadership was trying to think creatively about reaching out to these people with the gospel of Jesus Christ.*

*A presentation was made by the pastor regarding their proposals and then, as the saying goes, all hell broke loose. Dave had noticed before that sometimes in a meeting at work the tone was set by the first person who responded. Everyone else in a meeting could unconsciously feel as if the agenda was set not by the person presenting (which everyone assumed would be in favor of the proposal) but by the person who first responded. If that person was also in favor, the ball could keep on rolling in a general direction in favor as had initially been outlined by the presenter. If, however, the first person to speak was against the proposal, especially if they spoke with evident emotion, pain or hurt, then, well, Dave had found that pulling the meeting back from the brink was a task fit for heroes.*

*So it proved in this church meeting too. The chair turned the conversation over to the room after the pastor had made his presentation, and the first person who spoke was an elderly gentleman, no longer in formal leadership at the church because of his advanced age, but an elder statesman, much respected and honored. His tone was well-known to the church, having chaired many meetings before and having preached on occasion as well, so the people recognized the emotional texture of his voice. It almost sounded as if he were choking back tears. No one really remembered exactly what he had said, but what was evident to everyone, and lodged in their minds thereafter, was that he was passionate – and passionately opposed to the work for reasons that evidently were painful to him. The point he seemed to be making was that the set of proposals that were geared towards reaching out to the new community coming to the town were not really about that at all. In reality, he felt, they were overturning what the church had stood for all these years, and actually threatening key biblical principles about the church worship services and the church itself. He quoted a number of Bible verses (not all of which Dave saw as relevant to the topic under discussion, but which did give a semblance of biblical authority to what he was saying). Immediately, everyone realized that, by comparison, the pastor and the chair of the meeting had not been quoting very much from the Bible, but had instead been talking about statistics and opportunities, which now all seemed to be very much 'market speech', not 'Bible speech'.*

*Trouble was in the air.*

*The meeting went on for a couple of hours, but really (Dave knew) the chance of the leadership getting a unified consensus in favor of their proposals was dead as soon as that elderly gentleman had nearly cried when speaking in opposition. It might have been better if right then and there, they had gathered together, hugged each other, prayed and had come back in a month to talk again. But they didn't. They talked and talked. Tempers flared. Harsh words were spoken.*

*The next Sunday the pastor preached as normal, judiciously making no mention of the difficult meeting when he was speaking from the pulpit, but referencing a letter from the leaders to the congregation that was at the back of the church. When Dave read it, he realized that they were trying to make amends. They were offering anyone who had been hurt or confused to come* and talk with the leaders, and there would be another meeting in a month's time to reconsider whether the proposal for more outreach was how the Lord was leading at this time or not. Dave glanced down the letter and felt a little queasy. All this effort and for what gain?

That evening he picked up the Bible. He started to read through 1 Corinthians. Then he read 2 Corinthians. Wow. All this 'stuff' was not new. It was part of being sinners saved under grace living together in the new community. Dave wondered whether what really mattered was not the end goal – whether they adopted this program or that program or neither – but how they loved each other. With that in place, as they talked, then the whole spectrum of opportunities for forward progress would open up more and more.

He read through Ephesians. He noted how Paul in Ephesians 4 called God's people to make every effort to keep the unity of the Spirit. He also noted how that unity, as well as maturity, grew out of an increasing and deliberate focus on the Word of God. Dave resolved to continue to encourage the pastor as he preached from the Bible, and to study the Bible more himself.

Five years later Dave read over his journal that recorded all these details. It was amazing what had happened since as they had learnt to love each other and focus on the Word. God had done amazing things.

## Questions for discussion

**1.** Have you ever been in a Christian group or church which had unity problems? Why do you think this was?

**2.** Read through Ephesians 4. What do you think Paul says is the answer to growing unity and maturity?

**3.** Why do you think the Corinthian church had so much trouble with loving each other (1 Cor. 1:11)?

**4.** Read through 1 Corinthians 13. How could this be a rallying cry for church relationships today?

**5.** Jesus told his disciples that the greatest among them was 'servant of all' (Mark 9:35). Who is this servant of all? How could we all follow that example by living to serve each other?

**6.** One example Jesus used was foot washing (John 13:1-17). Why is this such a powerful illustration of what it means to love each other?

**7.** Is it encouraging to read through Acts and the New Testament letters and realize that the early Christians did not always get along together perfectly? How could we learn from their mistakes as well as imitate their excellences?

## QUESTION 8

# Should I go back if I have been hurt by church?

The obvious answer to that is 'yes', but it's more complicated than it may first appear to some people. If you've really been hurt by a church (and the word 'hurt' can cover a number of different realities, from minor to really quite extreme), the wounds that this creates are not susceptible to glib answers or easy solutions. Certainly, as the saying goes, 'It takes two to tango,' and if you've been hurt by a church, it may not be entirely their fault. On the other hand, I rarely have to do counseling with churches asking, 'What do we do when someone hurts us? 'There is an authority structure that churches represent – and to some extent still today possess – that gives them unique opportunities to bless people, and unique opportunities to not be a blessing as well.

Let's rationally consider the alternatives, first of all. What other alternative is there other than to try to go back to another church and start again?

Unlike other relationships, you can't just avoid church forever. If church is the local representation of the body of Christ, and if you are a member of Christ, you will be longing to be actually and practically reunited with that body of which you are truly and spiritually a part. You will not want to stay away forever. Somewhere deep down you will know this.

If, then, at some point you are going to want to re-enter church life, the next question is when and how? Here are my suggestions.

**1.** Don't just join *any* church. Some churches hurt people because they are not healthy churches. You want to join a church that not only says they follow Jesus, but actually does follow him. That means the Bible should be taught from the pulpit. That means that the gospel of Jesus Christ should be central to the church's life. That means that the church should not only be well-ordered and structured, with a healthy eldership or leadership, but a place of committed love, authentic discipleship and disciplined Christian living.

**2.** Guard your heart against *cynicism*. When you have been hurt, it is easy to throw up protective psychological barriers and be cynical about everything that seems to be occurring, to think to yourself, 'Oh, yeah, you *say* that, but I know what churches are *really* like.' Listen, no one in church claims to be perfect. In fact, the whole structure of a biblical church is proclaiming the message that only in Christ can we be saved. We know full well we are not perfect. There are plenty of sinners around here.

**3.** Practice a *biblical authenticity*. Being *authentic* does not mean being who you are without processing what you should be or trying to be who you should be. We need to aim to live up to our authentic self, not downgrade ourselves to an inauthentic, unfocused, lowest-common-denominator self.

The word 'authentic' holds the key to understanding this distinction: the *author* of the *authentic* self is not finally *you*, but actually *God*. So your true, authentic self is you as God has designed you to be. A jigsaw piece is not less authentic when it is joined to the other pieces in the puzzle, and it is not more authentic when it does not fit. A fish is not more authentic out of water than in water – out of water it is drowning. A person is not more authentic jumping out of a plane without a parachute – 'Look at me! I'm so *authentic!*' To be truly and genuinely authentic is to be who you are as designed by God.

**4.** Understand the difference between *friendship* and *fellowship*. To be in a church with other Christians means that you are called to love them. That does not mean that you are called to like them. A lot of people get hurt in church life because they misunderstand this distinction. They think that being in church means you have to like everyone around you and everyone has to like you. Not at all. There may well be some people in the church who you like, who can actually be your *friends*, but there is no reason to think that includes everyone. Church is family: you love your family, but sometimes you'd rather watch a baseball game with your friends. Some of your family are also your best friends. The two don't always go together. That's okay.

**5.** Don't *import* into your next church the baggage from your last church. That means not projecting onto people around you the stuff you have from the people at the last church. There may well be someone you need to say sorry to from your last church. That's one way to leave the bags from the last church and not bring them into the new church. You want a fresh start. You want a sense of starting over, not of a Groundhog Day – here we go again.

**6.** Take *commitment* slowly but steadily. When you've been hurt, you're a little gun-shy of commitment. This is understandable and completely normal. Perhaps you're someone who in the past tended to jump right in with both feet with hardly a second thought. Now you are not so sure. Well, don't run to extremes. Don't get into the habit of never committing. Take it slowly. Keep progressing steadily. Start with attending. Then find a small group. Then get involved with serving. Give of your time, your talent and your treasure. Bit by bit, slow but steady wins the race.

**7.** Guard your ultimate center of loyalty for no one else but Jesus. I've always been fascinated by John saying of Jesus that he did not entrust himself to people for he knew what was in them (John 2:24). You are called to love and serve people, and to be in fellowship with Christians. All this requires a degree of trust, commitment, loyalty and involvement. But it does not require the ultimate degree of trust. Only God is worthy of that sort of worship. Some people get hurt because they are really exposing the inner person to another human person, when the only person who can handle that level of vulnerability and tenderness is Jesus.

Look at it like the spokes of a wheel. As we are all joined to the hub, the spokes span out to the rim of the wheel, and the wheel spins effectively. Jesus is the relational hub of the church – not the pastor, not the small group leader, no other human. Keep Jesus in the center, and our love and commitment to one another grows as we are all connected in him.

## A story

*Sarah inched into the back of the church and sat down, glancing furtively around her. After the service had finished, she scurried out the back door,* shaking hands quickly with the minister, avoiding eye contact. The next week, though, she was there again. This time she was slightly less hasty in her departure after the service had finished, though she still did not stop for coffee or conversation. When someone smiled at her, she did not smile back. She looked suspicious.

She kept on coming, week after week, and gradually bit by bit her guard came down. This last Sunday when the minister shook her hand, she even replied to his greeting. As time went on the full story would emerge, some details of which are too sensitive to print, but the basic story was as follows.

Sarah had been a long-term member of a church in an adjoining community to the one where she was now attending church. She was scared that there would be people who would know her – or her parents. It was all she could do, she told people in the end, to not turn up wearing dark glasses and a hat. In fact, she was sure she would have done that if it would not have drawn even more attention to herself. Instead, she caked her face with makeup and kept her eyes firmly fixed on the floor.

In this other church where she had been for many years, and where her parents still worshiped, an event had occurred. In reality it was a series of events, but a series that culminated in a particular blow-up. She was hauled before the council at last and asked to give an account of what had taken place. Nervously, she told the whole story. Once the truth came out (as it so often does), just about everyone could see that what had taken place was not her fault, or at least no more her fault than anyone else's. She had behaved in a manner which, while certainly not perfect in itself, was understandable and how many a right thinking, genuinely Christian person might well behave in similar circumstances.

*Sarah had, in a sense, been vindicated. But though this was a great relief to her (not to mention to her parents), a strange thing occurred when she next attended the main service of the church. She felt exposed. The word 'sanctuary' kept on flashing across her mind's eye, and all she could think was that this space no longer felt safe. It did not seem like a 'sanctuary' from life's difficulties. Instead, it seemed like the place where she was more likely to be exposed, rather than a place where she would be protected. She kept on trying to attend, but eventually decided she should try something new.*

*As I say, the details related to 'the event' (as Sarah called it in her mind), as well as the whole series of events that led up that 'event', cannot be related in detail. But the upshot of it all was a deep hurt, a hidden anger and a fear related to church. Sarah was scared of being hurt again.*

*She covered up that fear well. She snapped at people if they tried to engage her in intimate conversation. She dressed dowdily, covering herself from head to toe with a sort of barrier to the outside world. She gave people her best 'hard stare' when they asked her questions. All in all, she had erected a pattern of behavior that was most likely to keep her safe, even in public spaces like church buildings, and also was most likely to keep her from developing new real friendships. It was a price worth paying, she was in effect deciding. Better to be safe than sorry, or hurt again.*

*Still Sarah kept coming back, week after week after week. She had not yet managed to pass more than a vague politeness with the minister at the back of the church after the service. But she had, just this last week, engaged one of the elderly ladies in the congregation in conversation. She seemed sweet, as well as wise. As Sarah talked to this elderly lady, she discovered that there were quite a few older folks in the church who were struggling to get to church as they could not drive any more, and some of them could not cook. Sarah wondered whether she might have found a niche, a place for her to serve.*

# Questions for discussion

1. Have you been hurt by a church?

2. Have you ever had to leave a church under a cloud?

3. What can you do to enter a church without taking baggage with you from previous church experiences?

4. If you have never been hurt by a church, have you ever hurt a church yourself?

5. How does Jesus' teaching about his disciples loving each other impact church relationships? How does Jesus' teaching about discipline impact church relationships?

6. How could you be on the lookout to include someone who has been hurt?

7. What sort of next steps could you take to re-engage, if necessary, with a local church?

# What should I look for in a healthy church?

This is the million dollar question in Christian circles, because what happens is most people who answer it effectively answer it by saying (more or less), 'Find a church like mine.' They don't quite come out and actually say, 'You're looking for a healthy church? What do you know, come and join ours!' But when you get right down to it, basically that is what they are saying.

Obviously, I do think our church is healthy (otherwise, I would pretty rapidly be doing something about it). So that means that I also will be saying, in one way or another, healthy churches are like our church. But there are other types of churches that are healthy in other ways. Furthermore, there are parts of our church life where we need to grow still.

By God's grace and mercy, though, there is in our church culture a commitment to core convictions that tend historically to maintain gospel health in a church. I would name five matters:

First, a thorough commitment to the prevalence and prominence of the gospel of Jesus Christ.

Second, a thorough commitment to the actual teaching of the Bible and its functional and genuine authority over all matters.

Third, a Biblical involvement in each other's lives through life and fellowship and community.

Fourth, a thorough commitment to reach out with that gospel to those around us, locally and globally, to be part of God's mission for the whole world.

Fifth, a biblical commitment to authentic, Word-driven, Spirit-filled worship around the biblical trajectory of the gospel.

On those five things we still have much to grow in and learn, for sure, but I think they are pretty hardwired into who we are.

That is what you are looking for in a healthy church: *Gospel FLOW*. That is, the gospel driving forward Fellowship (F), Learning (L), Outreach (O) and Worship (W). Basically, it's all about the gospel. The gospel is not just the ABC of the Christian life; it is the A–Z, as Christ is the Alpha and the Omega, the beginning and the end (Rev. 22:13). Each of the four core values is driven forward by that gospel and expresses that gospel in various ways. At our church we want to become a church of gospel excellence to change the world. Our understanding of this comes out of many passages in the Bible, but especially Acts 2:42-47:

They devoted themselves to the apostles' teaching and to fellowship, to the breaking of bread and to prayer. Everyone was filled with awe at the many wonders and signs performed by the apostles. All the believers were together and had everything in common. They sold property and possessions to give to anyone who had need. Every day they continued to meet together in the temple courts. They broke bread in their homes and ate together with glad and sincere hearts, praising God and enjoying the favor of all the people. And the Lord added to their number daily those who were being saved.

There are certainly plenty of other ways of expressing these convictions of what church is about that you find throughout the Bible (another passage to study would be Hebrews 12 and 13). You can give this approach different names and it can be expressed in various ways, but one way or another the kind of things you are looking for in a healthy church, and looking to further in a healthy church, are those five areas listed above.

Of course there is another side to this question, which is not so much 'What am I looking for in a healthy church?' but more, 'How can I contribute to make this church more healthy?' To do that:

**1.** Support your leaders.

**2.** Be committed in your attendance at worship services.

**3.** Give regularly, consistently and joyfully with generosity of your money, your time and your commitment to the work of the gospel in the church.

**4.** Find ways to serve in the church.

**5.** Find ways to tell others about the church and live a life whereby you are inviting people to Jesus and to church.

**6.** Forgive others quickly, do not bear grudges, love and have mercy.

**7.** Live a life of gospel holiness, that is, pursuing Christ with all you have, loving him above all else, and loving your neighbor as yourself. Be devoted to regular Bible reading and prayer, take care of your family spiritually if you have one and turn your household into a place of godliness and Christlikeness, so that church is not just one day in seven, but a seven-day-a-week, 365-day-a-year living experience.

With a healthy church and increasingly healthy people involved – the church, under God's grace and only by his favor, as it remains committed to Christ and his Word, will organically, gradually become more like Christ and more effective at his mission to the world.

That's not just health. It's life, vitality and dynamism.

## A story

*Brian was excited at the thought of discovering God's people. Unlike many people in the West, he had had very little exposure at all to any form of Christianity. Bizarrely, his parents had actually brought him up as a lesser member of a very small Wiccan sect, and so his familiarity with the traditions of Christian churches was minimal at best. Fortunately for Brian, his parents also had a very high view of education, had taught him to think well and had done everything they could to send him to the best schools available. They wanted him to think, and think Brian did.*

*It was not too long before Brian began to meet some uncomfortable truths while he was at university. He had always known that his background was a tad unusual, but it had not occurred to him quite how unusual it really was. So far he had not yet met any other members of the same Wiccan sect at his university. In fact, he was not sure there were any other members at any of the universities that he had applied to attend. He felt alone – not ostracized, because everyone was kind and friendly to him – but definitely an odd man out.*

*That sense of estrangement by itself would not have been enough to have caused Brian to rethink his propositions. He had been well-versed in the fact that truth is not decided by a democratic vote, and it did not overly concern him that so few people believed what he believed. If anything, it made him concerned for them, and he wanted to be able to reach out to them and explain the mysteries of his Wiccan coven. No, it was not that what he believed was unusual that began to bother Brian, it was that – it rapidly became clear – it was blatantly and simply wrong. Brian had been taught to think, and as he had been given the tools that come with a higher education to be able to think at a different level, the tenets of his unusual Wiccan sect soon appeared not simply bizarre but downright duplicitous.*

*To cut a long story short, Brian was then introduced to a Christian group at his university. He began to study the Bible. Before long he had encountered Christ for himself. The man from Nazareth walked off the pages of Scripture and entered his life as the Lord of the galaxy. Brian was now, in other words, a Christian.*

*The next step was to find a church.*

*He tried the closest first. Not wanting to settle for second best, he then tried the next nearest. As a logical person, and without any theological guardrails by which to direct him, he decided he would simply try them all out one after the other, following a concentric circle moving out from his dormitory room.*

*In some ways they were all very similar – or at least all very different from what he had experienced growing up as a gathering of the supernatural. They read from the Bible. They prayed. They sang songs. Someone gave a talk based (sometimes more closely, sometimes frankly rather loosely) on a passage or passages from the Bible.*

*One day Brian walked into a church where the pastor did not simply announce his best idea for the day and talk about it, but explained carefully and applied relevantly the Scripture passage itself. He had the same experience of the man from Nazareth walking off the pages of Scripture and reaffirming his rightful rule over his heart and that of the entire universe. Brian was hooked.*

## Questions for discussion

1. What in your view goes into making a 'healthy' church?

2. Of those elements, which do you regard as the most important?

3. Does your church practice these elements that go into making a church healthy?

4. If not, are there other churches nearby which do?

5. Why is it important to be part of a healthy church?

6. Do you think any church is perfect? How can you avoid criticizing church and instead join an imperfect, but still healthy local church?

## QUESTION 10

# How can I serve in a church?

Here is what *not* to do. Don't come to a meeting or into a church gathering of some kind and offer what you think of as your very best gift or ability and insist that it comes to the forefront, no matter what anyone else says. 'Dear brother, perhaps your gift is *not* singing in the worship team/praise band/choir.' Or, 'Dear brother, you might be better off rethinking whether God has *really* told you to preach, or whether in fact you might be better off helping out in the sound booth to help someone else preach instead.' Or equivalent conversations of various kinds that I have had on innumerable occasions with people whose perceptions of what they are good at don't quite match reality.

The issue is that in church life we try to be loving, but what that means, though, is that sometimes we don't quite shoot straight with each other. If they went to a recording studio in Nashville with that voice they probably wouldn't get past the first round of interviews. But, hey, it's church, so sure we'll inflict their loud, off-key singing on the rest of us.

It's much better, though, to actually speak the truth in love and tell each other what we perceive are each other's gifts. There needs to be a level of community discernment that rubs against the grain of our individualism. The 'niceness' culture of some churches can prevent striving for excellence in all things. There is a more biblical way to love each other. We want round pegs in round holes, not round pegs in square holes. That's better for the holes, but it's also better for the pegs, too.

So how do you serve in church life? The answer is that word *SERVE*. Let me break it down for us.

**S** – Start Small. You want to look around and ask yourself not 'What can I do that's really cool?' but 'What can I do to help out?' It will usually be pretty obvious because someone will be asking for people to volunteer in some area or another. He who is faithful in small things will have larger things with which to be faithful before too long. But Start Small.

**E** – Every Endeavor. We want you to have enough time for friends, family, and neighbors, but if we are honest with each other (as I hope we are), most of our time in life goes towards TV or junky internet surfing. We all have more time than we really let on that we do. That's why when a country goes to war suddenly there is more time for people to do things. There is a sense of focus and effort. We are in a spiritual war. William Gurnall, the great Puritan writer and author of *The Christian in Complete Armour*, encouraged believers to sleep with their 'armor' on. In other words, don't be too picky about what you do. Get involved, give of your time. Every Endeavor.

**R** – Real Relationships. Part of the great side benefit of serving alongside other people is that you get to know them. This is how in God's design the church works, as each part of the body does its job. We get to know each other. We work alongside and start to relate to each other as three-dimensional beings. People will be far more likely to open up to you as you serve together side-by-side. Embrace this opportunity for developing Real Relationships with others in the church family.

**V** – Virtual Virtue. I don't mean pretend virtue. I mean that we want people who serve to do so in a spirit of commitment to Christ, godliness of lifestyle and biblical faithfulness, but we do not expect anyone to be perfect. None of us is perfect, not a single one. We are all sinners, even the Christians, even the pastors. We do not expect perfection. What we expect from all of us is a growing commitment to Christlikeness fuelled by the power of the gospel in the power of the Spirit. We expect quick forgiveness of each other when we fail. We expect the quick ability to ask for forgiveness, and the equally quick acceptance. We live in a community of the forgiven, not a community of the perfect, and we strive to become more and more like Christ, until one day our Virtual Virtue will be perfected as we are made fully like Christ and share in his glory. In the meantime it's virtually and increasingly virtuous.

**E** – Exceptionally Excellent. This is church. That does *not* mean second best is good enough. We are talking about serving the living God. That means only the best is good enough. What we should bring to our service at church is better than what would be required at the most elite university, the most successful multinational business, the highest ranking sports team in the National Basketball Association. Part of exceptional excellence is loving people despite their weaknesses. We make mistakes; of course, that is understood. But we aim for exceptional excellence – in everything, all the time. That means exceptionally loving those who are broken – because that is excellence as defined by the gospel. It means that we have people from all sorts of backgrounds in the church – because that is the most excellent way of love as the Bible describes it. It also means that what we do is done with first-rate excellence because we do it for God. We aim to be Exceptionally Excellent.

All this is because serving in church is to *SERVE* in church. Certainly, we will find fulfillment as we do. Certainly, we will discover our gifts and capabilities as we do: our God-given gifts that he has invested in us for his glory. Certainly, we will find ways to continue to grow in these capabilities. But it all starts with this basic attitude that shapes our service, our volunteering: namely *SERVE*.

After all, even Jesus came to serve, not to be served (Matt. 20:28).

## A story

*Jill had always loved music. On her iTunes playlist she had a wide range of music, quite an eclectic taste from rock to classical to jazz and several other genres like country, too. Jill always said that there was not a kind of music that she did not like. She listened to the tribal music derived from anthropological studies in Africa in the early days. She listened to chamber music. She liked the whole thing – guitar, kazoo, choir, the whole lot.*

*Jill also loved to sing. She sang in the bath. She sang in the shower. She sang in the car when she pumped her music as loud as she could. She whistled when she walked down the country paths on her Sunday afternoon strolls, and she whistled when she cycled to work. In short, Jill was a music person.*

*Except, she had never really learnt to play anything. She was now in her mid-twenties and she felt it was probably too late to take up a musical instrument now, at least to manage to excel at any of them with any kind of seriousness. But she knew she loved to sing. So instead, she offered herself to the person leading the music at her church.*

*He was all smiles and offered to meet her for an audition. There were, in fact, several key performances coming up when, quite frankly, he could do with a few more strong female voices. He was excited to hear what she could offer. Jill felt nervous about an audition and told the music director as much, but he assured her that he was not looking for perfection and pretty much anyone could serve in this area of the church. It was just to give him a sense of the right place to fit her into in the church.*

*The day of the audition began, and the music director asked Jill if there was a song she would like to sing. Thinking quickly, she decided that perhaps she should pick a very well-known Christian song, and so she offered to sing 'Amazing Grace'. Smiling broadly, the music director began to play the tune to the great hymn, and when he had introduced it, looked across at Jill, nodded to indicate (Jill assumed) that it was her time to sing.*

*Jill began: 'Amazing grace, how sweet the sound, that saved a wretch like me …'*

*The music director interrupted. 'Okay', he said, 'don't worry, you're probably just nervous. Let's take it from the top again.' He played the introduction to the hymn and once more nodded to her, and Jill began to sing from the start of the song again: 'Amazing grace, how sweet the sound, that saved a wretch like me, I once was lost, but now am found, was blind but now I see.'*

*Jill carried on singing, having long ago learnt all the verses by heart, and the music director carried on playing. But something did not seem quite right.*

*'Okay', he said at the end, 'well, I think we might have a problem. How long have you been singing?'*

*'All my life', Jill replied.*

*'And have you ever sung in a group or in a band or choir before?' he asked.*

*'No', Jill said. 'This will be my first time.' She tried to smile but found that she was so nervous now that she could not.*

*The music director looked at her. 'This is the toughest part of my job', he said, 'but I wonder if you've heard of the phrase "tone deaf".' Jill had.*

*'Well', said the music director, 'you're not tone deaf. You obviously enjoy music, but you are what I call "tune deaf". It's not that you didn't hit all the notes. It's that the notes and you weren't even in the same room.'*

*'If you like', he carried on, 'I could refer you to someone who can teach singing. He says that anyone can be trained to sing. I believe him. You might like to do that. Or you might like to think whether there's another area in the church where you could serve instead.'*

*Jill went away disconsolate. She appreciated the music director's honesty, so she wasn't angry, but she wondered what it was that she could do instead. A few moments later the music director called her on the phone. 'You know what?' he said. 'I heard that you are the executive director at ...' (and he named a local business). 'Is that right?'*

*'Yes', she said.*

'Well, that's quite a remarkably senior position for your age. If you still want to be involved in music, I wonder whether instead I can ask you to help me get organized. You see, I can sing, but I need someone to manage all the details. To be frank, we're in a bit of chaos over here in the choir room.'

Jill smiled to herself. 'Ah', she thought, 'so that's what you had in mind' – talking this time to God.

## Questions for discussion

1.  Have you ever done a 'gift survey' that is designed to help you discover what sort of gifts you have?

2.  What sort of strengths and weaknesses do your closest friends say that you have?

3.  When someone expresses appreciation for you, what kind of things do they most often point out?

4.  If there was a need in the church, even if it was not related to something that you particularly enjoyed, would it be right to volunteer?

5.  Think of someone who seems to be in their 'sweet spot'? What do you suppose that experience is like?

6.  How could you serve in your local church?

# Conclusion

As we come to the end of this book let us conclude by asking ourselves whether we are ready now to be church men and women. We have talked about what makes a church a true church, and what we can do to help a true church become a healthy church. We are not to feel any sense of guilt or unease about leaving 'churches' that are not truly *churches*. Far from it: come out and be separate! If a church is *not* a true church of God, then why continue anymore? Don't feel guilty; feel propelled to find a church that is a true church.

On the other hand, we are to be wary of any sense of divisiveness, superiority or arrogance with relation to a true church that perhaps is still unhealthy, or needs to grow in healthiness. We all have room to grow and develop as individuals and as churches.

But given some of the definitions and discussions that have already taken place in this book – answers to the ten most common questions about church – the best way we can honestly conclude this book is by asking ourselves whether we are now ready to be church men and women.

I have two Bible passages I wish to mention in this regard. The first is a *motivation*. The second is a *vision*.

## Motivation

The first passage is in Acts 20:28, where Paul describes the church as that which God 'bought with his own blood'.

Think about that statement.

Think again.

Think some more.

*Bought with his own blood.* So when we discuss the church, we are talking about that for which God in Christ shed his blood. If nothing could be more precious to the Christian than the blood of Jesus, what kind of value are we to place on the church that cost him that blood?

As I say, this is quite a *motivation* to be church men and women. When we are discussing the church, we are not *merely* discussing a building where a church meets, a leadership group that runs a particular kind of church, or even the people that go to making up a church. We are discussing something for which God in Christ gave his own blood.

If that does not motivate us, what will? Church is so important, so central, that God in Christ was willing to die for it. Should we not also be willing, therefore, to be church men and women?

## Vision

The second passage is a vision. It lies in a comparison of the first of Luke's three vignettes of the early church in Acts 2:42-47, with one secular ruler's description of the impact of this church upon the world in Acts 17:6. This church, he says, is the church that has 'turned the world upside down' (ESV). This is more than a *motivation*: it is a *vision*.

When we think of church and the value of us investing our time, talent and treasure in it, we are not only motivated by the realization that the church is something for which Christ died, we are also given vision by realizing that the New Testament is God's agency for changing the world. We say it like this: 'Growing a church of gospel excellence to change the world.'

So, you want to see healthy families?

You want to see people come to worship Jesus?

You want to see the disadvantaged given hope and meaning?

You want to see lives changed and brought back from the brink of depression and disappointment?

You want to see societies reformed?

You want to see revival?

You want to see prisons emptied, feuds forgotten, enemies become friends?

You want to see resources (time, talent and treasure) released for gospel purposes?

You want – in short – to change the world for good for God's glory? The agent for that change is a growing church of gospel excellence.

If you are ready, then, to be a church man or woman, or to grow in that commitment, why not take the following covenant (or one like it) as yours? Drawn from a local church covenant, these are the kinds of words that are normally said in a question and response form with a whole group covenanting together in a local church:

I do now acknowledge the covenant of Christian consecration of myself and all that I have to the service of God; I do covenant with a true biblical church to love her in the Lord, to submit to the government and discipline of Christ's church as there administered. And further I agree to live as a humble Christian in regular attendance upon the services of public worship of this church; to give regularly of my means for the support of Christian work; to maintain private and family prayer; to give diligent heed to the Word of God, ever more fully yielding my life to the indwelling Christ, that the fruit of the Spirit may be manifested in me.